Supporting Phonics and Spelling

FOR AGES 8–9

Andrew Brodie

Contents

Andrew Brodie: Supporting Phonics & Spelling © A & C Black Publishers Ltd. 2006

Introduction

Supporting Phonics and Spelling is aimed at children in mainstream classrooms who have been identified as needing 'additional' or 'different' literacy support, particularly in phonics and spelling. The activities can be used by anyone working with children who fall into this category, whether you are a teacher, classroom assistant or parent.

Typically the eight to nine year-old children for whom the book is intended will be working at the levels expected of Year 2 or Year 3, or may simply need extra help in tackling the level of work appropriate for Year 4. Their difficulties may be short-term, and could be overcome with extra practice and support on a one-to-one or small group basis, or they may be long-term, where such support enables them to make progress but at a level behind their peer group.
The activities in this book provide exactly what these children need – systematic repetition and practice of early phonic skills, based on a strong foundation of synthetic phonics and the best features of analytic phonics.
The *Supporting Phonics and Spelling* series reflects the best practice in teaching spelling through phonics. It provides an approach that is:

- Systematic
- Multi-sensory
- Based on speaking and listening
- Linked closely to reading skills

This book is organised into three-page sets. It is vital that the teaching assistant or class teacher reads the 'Teacher's notes' on 'Sheet a' before starting the lesson. This first page in each set introduces specific phonemes and provides a good opportunity for the teacher and child to sound them out together. Children can also use their multi-sensory skills at this stage by drawing the letters in sand or making them out of dough or modelling clay. The second worksheet revises the same phonemes, but with a particular emphasis on speaking, listening and writing. The final worksheet in the set features a list of words containing the phonemes for further practice and consolidation. When used together, the three worksheets provide a thorough grounding in the phonic knowledge and skills that children need for confident reading, writing and spelling.

All the worksheets can be used on their own or alongside other literacy schemes that are already established within your school. The activities are simple and self-explanatory and the instruction text is deliberately kept to a minimum to make the pages easy to use for adults and less daunting for children to follow.

We recommend that the children use the *Supporting Phonics and Spelling* worksheets on a daily basis for approximately 20 minutes. Regular practice of previous learning is an integral part of the series. In completing the activities, teachers should place particular emphasis on speaking and listening skills. Most of the three-page sets include the opportunity to use dictation, a teaching method that may be considered old-fashioned, but when used appropriately can be both fun and rewarding. Opportunities will arise to dictate sounds, whole words and whole sentences. Initially, pupils might need help with each of these but will soon gain confidence as they experience increasing and visible success.

Children generally achieve the greatest success in an atmosphere of support and encouragement. Praise from a caring adult can be the best reward for the children's efforts. The worksheets and activities in this book will provide many opportunities for children to enjoy these successes. The development of a positive attitude and the resulting increase in self-esteem will help them with all of their schoolwork.

Definitions and explanations of terms

(Please note that some publications will give slightly different definitions.)

Phoneme

A phoneme is a unit of sound and can be represented by:
one letter e.g. /b/ as in **b**at two letters e.g. /ee/ as in sw**ee**t
three letters e.g. /ear/ as in n**ear**
Note that a phoneme can be represented in several different ways
e.g. the sound /ee/ can be represented by:

ee as in f**ee**t	**ei** as in c**ei**ling	**ie** as in ch**ie**f
ea as in n**ea**t	**i** as in sk**i**	**e_e** as in P**e**t**e**

Vowel phoneme

A vowel phoneme makes an open sound and always contains at least one vowel –
you usually have to open your mouth to say it.
Examples of vowel phonemes are:

/a/ as in b**a**t	/ie/ as in cr**ie**s	/oo/ as in b**oo**k
/ur/ as in t**ur**n	/ow/ as in t**ow**n	

Consonant phoneme

A consonant phoneme always contains at least one consonant and usually involves
closing the mouth, or 'biting' the lower lip, or touching the roof of the mouth with
the tongue. (There are exceptions e.g. /h/). Examples of consonant phonemes are:

/b/ as in **b**at	/f/ as in **ph**otograph
/th/ as in **th**ey	/ng/ as in si**ng**

Grapheme

A grapheme is a letter, a pair of letters or a group of letters representing a single
sound e.g. **ee**, **ei**, **ie**, **ea**, **i** and **e_e** are all graphemes representing the sound /ee/.

Grapheme/phoneme correspondence

The relationship between letters and the sounds that they represent.

Digraph

A digraph consists of two letters representing a single sound. So, for example, the
grapheme **ch** is a consonant digraph because it is made up of two consonants.
The grapheme **ee** is a vowel digraph and although it contains a consonant, **ow** is
also a vowel digraph, because it makes an open sound like a vowel does.

Split digraph

A split digraph consists of two vowels separated by a consonant to make one
phoneme e.g. **e_e** as in P**e**t**e** **i_e** as in m**i**n**e** **a_e** as in c**a**m**e**

Trigraph

A trigraph is a group of three letters representing a single sound.
The vowel phonemes /air/ and /ear/ are trigraphs.

Cluster

A cluster consists of two or more letters making more than one sound. For example:
t **h** **r** are three letters that can make the cluster **thr**, which
consists of the phonemes /th/ and /r/.

Blending

Blending is the process of combining different sounds (phonemes) to be able to say
a particular word or to make up part of a word e.g.
/sh/ /i/ /p/ can be blended to make the word ship.

/th/ /r/ are blended to make the cluster **thr**. Sometimes a cluster like this
will be called a blend.

Segmenting

Segmenting is the process of splitting a word into its different phonemes to be able
to spell it e.g. **ship** can be segmented into the three phonemes /sh/ /i/ /p/.

Onset and rime

The terms 'onset' and 'rime' are used together when analysing words. For example,
in the word 'cat' the phoneme represented by the letter 'c' is described as the onset
and the final cluster 'at' is described as the rime. Note that words that end with a
particular rime always rhyme but words that rhyme do not always contain the same
rime! For example, cat, rat and bat all end with the rime 'at' and
all rhyme. But the words tough and muff rhyme but have
the rimes 'ough' and 'uff'.

vc

vowel/consonant e.g. the word *it*

cv

consonant/vowel e.g. the word *be*

cvc

consonant/vowel/consonant e.g. the word *cat*

ccvc

consonant/consonant/vowel/consonant e.g. the word *shop*

cvcc

consonant/vowel/consonant/consonant e.g. the word *fast*

Andrew Brodie: Supporting Phonics & Spelling © A & C Black Publishers Ltd. 2006

An introduction to phonemes

Language can be analysed by considering the separate sounds that combine to make up spoken words. These sounds are called phonemes and the English language has more than forty of them. It is possible to concentrate on forty-two main phonemes but here we list forty-four phonemes including those that are commonly used only in some regions of the country.

It is helpful to look at each phoneme individually and then at some sample words that demonstrate how the phoneme is represented by different graphemes as shown in the list below. Try reading each word out loud to spot the phoneme in each one. For the simple vowel sounds the graphemes are shown in bold text.

Vowel phonemes	Sample words
/a/	b**a**t
/e/	l**e**g, g**ue**ss, h**ea**d, s**ai**d, s**ay**s
/i/	b**i**g, plant**e**d, b**u**sy, cr**y**stal, d**e**cide, **e**xact, g**u**ilt, r**e**peat
/o/	d**o**g, **ho**nest, w**a**s, qu**a**rrel, tr**ou**gh, v**au**lt, **yach**t (the ch is silent)
/u/	b**u**g, l**o**ve, bl**oo**d, c**o**mfort, r**ou**gh, y**ou**ng
/ae/	rain, day, game, navy, weigh, they, great, rein
/ee/	been, team, field, these, he, key, litre, quay, suite
/ie/	pie, high, sign, my, bite, child, guide, guy, haiku
/oe/	boat, goes, crow, cone, gold, sew
/ue/	soon, do, July, blue, chew, June, bruise, shoe, you, move, through
/oo/	book, put
/ar/	barn, bath (regional), laugh (regional), baa, half, clerk, heart, guard
/ur/	Thursday, girl, her, learn, word
/or/	born, door, warm, all, draw, cause, talk, aboard, abroad, before, four, bought, taught
/ow/	brown, found, plough
/oi/	join, toy, buoy
/air/	chair, pear, care, where, their, prayer
/ear/	near, cheer, here, weird, pier

Try saying this vowel phoneme in the sample words:

/er/   fast**er**, g**a**zump, curr**a**nt, wooll**e**n, circ**us**

Not to be confused with the phoneme /ur/, this phoneme is very similar to /u/ but is slightly different in some regions.

Consonant phonemes with sample words

/b/	bag, rub
/d/	dad, could
/f/	off, calf, fast, graph, tough
/g/	ghost, girl, bag
/h/	here, who
/j/	bridge, giraffe, huge, jet
/k/	kite, antique, cat, look, quiet, choir, sock, six (note that the sound made by the letter x is a blend of the phonemes /k/ and /s/)
/l/	leg, crawl, full
/m/	mug, climb, autumn
/n/	now, gnash, knight, sign, fun
/p/	peg, tap
/r/	run, wrote
/s/	cinema, goose, listen, psalm, scene, see, sword, yes, less
/t/	ten, sit, receipt
/v/	vest, love
/w/	wet
/wh/	when (regional)
/y/	yes
/z/	choose, was, zoo
/th/	the, with
/th/	thank, path
/ch/	cheer, such, match
/sh/	shop, rush, session, chute
/zh/	usual
/ng/	thing, think

For some phonemes you may dispute some of the examples that we have listed. This may be due to regional variations in pronunciation. Disputing the sounds is a positive step as it ensures that you are analysing them!

It is not necessary to teach the children all the graphemes for each phoneme but to be ready and aware when pupils suggest words to you to represent a particular sound. They are not wrong with their suggestions and should be praised for recognising the phoneme. You can then show them how the words that they have suggested are written but that normally the particular sound is represented by a specific grapheme.

Andrew Brodie: Supporting Phonics & Spelling © A & C Black Publishers Ltd. 2006

Examining the list of high frequency words

These words from the high frequency list for Years 1 and 2 are still very relevant as they do not always follow simple phonic patterns, although all of them include phonic elements that follow a typical pattern. Children will find them easier to tackle through developing the phonic skills that we are encouraging in this series of books: listening to sounds, speaking the sounds clearly and segmenting words into sounds that can be matched to appropriate letters, i.e. matching phonemes to appropriate graphemes.

about	called	has	love	old	sister	twenty
after	came	have	made	once	so	two
again	can't	help	make	one	some	us
an	could	her	man	or	take	very
another	did	here	many	our	ten	want
as	dig	him	may	out	than	way
back	do	his	more	over	that	were
ball	don't	home	much	people	their	what
be	door	house	must	pull	them	when
because	down	how	name	push	then	where
bed	first	if	new	put	there	who
been	from	jump	next	ran	these	will
blue	girl	just	night	red	three	with
boy	good	last	nine	saw	time	would
brother	got	laugh	not	school	too	you
but	had	little	now	seen	took	
by	half	lived	off	should	twelve	

Some of these words are included in the phonic lists in this book and some are included as 'odd ones out'. You may like to introduce other words from the list as opportunities arise, supporting the children in segmenting the words to be able to spell them. Below is the list of focus words that appear in this book, though many others are included within the activities.

about	kit	scribble	snake	spot	swan	twin
been	kite	scrub	snap	spotted	swap	twirl
bit	light	scuff	sneeze	spotting	sweep	twist
bite	made	scum	sniff	spray	sweet	two
broke	make	shred	snip	spread	swim	use
cake	might	shredded	snow	spring	swing	used
came	nose	shredding	snug	sprinkle	swoop	why
cried	note	shrill	space	squabble	take	woke
cries	now	shrink	space	square	thread	
cry	paper	shrub	spark	squash	three	
cube	right	shrug	speed	squeak	threw	
down	rude	sigh	spell	squeal	thrill	
fight	scalp	sight	spend	squeeze	throat	
flute	scamp	sit	spill	squid	through	
fright	scar	site	spin	squirt	throw	
game	scoop	slope	spinning	straw	tight	
globe	scoot	small	spit	stray	tried	
going	scooter	smart	spitting	stream	tries	
good	scrabble	smash	splash	street	try	
high	scramble	smell	splendid	strike	tube	
home	scrap	smile	splinter	string	tweet	
home	scrape	smoke	split	strong	twelve	
joke	scream	smooth	spoon	struggle	twenty	
June	screen	snail	sport	swam	twig	

1a	**Learning objective**	
	Phonemes **Consonants:** /b/,/k/,/f/,/s/,/t/ **Vowels:** /ie/,/i/	**Target words** kit, sit, bit, kite, site, sight, bite, fight

Teacher's notes

Worksheet 1a

- Photocopy this page and ask the child to cut out the target words.

- Ask him/her to identify the sounds (phonemes) in some of the words, the /k/, /i/ and /t/ in the word *kit*, for example.

- Discuss the words and what each word means. Help the child to read them by blending the phonemes. Draw his/her attention to the words *site* and *sight*, helping the child to see the difference between the two words and to understand their different meanings, even though they sound exactly the same.

Worksheet 1b

- Dictate the following words to the child to enable him/her to create the word bank: **kit, sit, bit, kite, site, sight, bite, fight**. S/he may need some help in segmenting each word into its phonemes to make it easier to spell. Say each word repeatedly and slowly, encouraging the child to hear the separate sounds.

- Help the child sort the words into the two boxes. Help him/her to identify the short vowel sounds and long vowel sounds. Comparing *kit* to *kite* and *sit* to *site* will help the child to observe the effect of the final **e** making the letter **i** 'say its own name'. The grapheme **igh** is a special way of creating the phoneme /ie/. Can the children think of other words that use this spelling to create the sound? E.g. *right, bright, light, high, sigh, flight*. Some of these words are included in Set 2. You could also ask the children if they can think of other words that contain the /ie/ sound where there is a final **e**, e.g. *time, nice, five, mine, nine*, etc.

- Now discuss the sentence shown on this worksheet : *Tom works on a building site.* It would be valuable to point out that the sentence starts with a capital letter and ends with a full stop but that, of course, the name *Tom* would start with a capital letter wherever it occurs.

- The word *building* includes the short vowel phoneme /i/ in two places but is special in that the first grapheme for this phoneme is **ui**. Help the child write extra sentences. Encourage him/her to write clearly, following the school's handwriting policy for letter formation, and to start the sentences with a capital letter, and to end them with a full stop.

Worksheet 1c

- This sheet includes the eight target words with the long vowel phoneme /ie/ or the short vowel phoneme /i/.

- This sheet could be copied for display purposes but it can also be used to provide the child with extra practice in writing the words. There are three writing lines for each word, enabling the child to use large and smaller writing. You could write each word on the first of the two smaller writing lines so that the child can copy your writing in the correct style used by your school.

TARGET WORDS

kit	sit	bit	kite
site	sight	bite	fight

Name: _____ **Date:** _____

Listen to your teacher. Write the words in the word bank.

WORD BANK

_____   _____   _____

_____   _____   _____

_____

Short i words	**Long i words**
_____	_____
_____	_____
_____	_____
	_____
	_____

★ Here is a sentence using one of the words.

    Tom works on a building site.

      capital letter   *full stop*

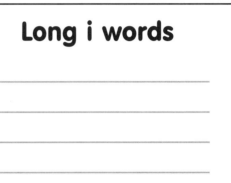

★ Write sentences using three of the other words.

_____

_____

_____

_____

_____

Andrew Brodie: Supporting Phonics & Spelling © A & C Black Publishers Ltd. 2006

Name: **Date:**

Words for today

kit

sit

kite

site

sight

bite

fight

bit

Andrew Brodie: Supporting Phonics & Spelling © A & C Black Publishers Ltd. 2006

2a

Phonemes
Consonants: /s/,/h/,/r/,/f/,/t/,/m/,/l/,/b/
Vowels: /ie/,/a/,/ow/

Target words
sigh, high, right, fright,
tight, might, light, about

Teacher's notes

Worksheet 2a

- Photocopy this page and ask the child to cut out the target words.

- Discuss the words and what each word means. Help the child to read them by blending the phonemes. Ask him/her to identify the sounds in some of the words, the /r/, /ie/ and /t/ in the word *right*, for example. Point out that the word *about* is the 'odd one out'.

Worksheet 2b

- Read the two introductory sentences with the child. Help him/her write two words for the **igh** list and four words for the **ight** list. You could dictate the words **sigh, high, right, tight, might, light,** repeating them slowly and carefully to encourage the child to segment each word into its phonemes to make spelling easier.

- Now discuss the sentence: *The boy had a terrible fright.* It would be valuable to point out that the sentence starts with a capital letter and ends with a full stop. The word *terrible* includes the short vowel phoneme /i/ and the consonant phoneme /l/ represented by the common grapheme **le**. Help the child write extra sentences. Encourage him/her to write clearly, following the school's handwriting policy for letter formation, and to start each sentence with a capital letter and to end it with a full stop.

Worksheet 2c

- This sheet includes the seven target words with the grapheme **igh** in each one, together with an extra word, *about*. The extra word is a useful high frequency word and can be used for an 'odd one out' activity. This sheet could be copied for display purposes but can also be used to provide the child with extra practice in writing the words. There are three writing lines for each word, enabling the child to use large and smaller writing. You could write each word on the first of the two smaller writing lines so that the child can copy your writing in the correct style used by your school.

TARGET WORDS

| sigh | high | right | fright |
| tight | might | light | about |

Name: **Date:**

Some **igh** words have a letter **t**:   **right**

Some **igh** words do not have a letter **t**:   **sigh**

★ Write two **igh** words: _____   _____

★ Write four **ight** words: _____   _____

          _____   _____

★ Look at this sentence.

   The boy had a terrible fright.

★ Write three sentences with an **igh** or **ight** word in each.

_____

_____

_____

_____

_____

Andrew Brodie: Supporting Phonics & Spelling © A & C Black Publishers Ltd. 2006

2c

Name: _____ **Date:** _____

Words for today

sigh _____ _____

high _____ _____

right _____ _____

fright _____ _____

tight _____ _____

might _____ _____

light _____ _____

about _____ _____

3a

Learning objective

Phonemes
Consonants: /k/ (as grapheme c),/r/,/d/,/z/, /wh/,/t/,/b/,/n/
Vowels: /ie/,/ee/

Target words
cry, cries, cried, try, tries, tried, why, been

Teacher's notes

Worksheet 3a

- Photocopy this page and ask the child to cut out the target words.

- Discuss the words and what each word means. Help the child to read them by blending the phonemes. Ask him/her to identify the sounds in some of the words, the /k/, /r/, /ie/ and /z/ in the word *cries*, for example. Point out that the word *been* is the 'odd one out'.

Worksheet 3b

- Discuss the sounds made by the letters at the top of the page concentrating first on the consonant phonemes and then on the vowel phonemes. Point out that the letter **s** can say /s/ or /z/. Note also that the letter **y** is acting as the vowel phoneme /ie/.

- Dictate the words **cry, cries, cried, try, tries, tried, why, been** for the child to write. You may need to repeat each word several times, making sure that the phonemes are pronounced clearly, to help the child to segment the word for spelling. Showing the target words to the child and then covering them while you dictate the words can be a very effective technique. It is important that the child is fully supported and gains lots of praise where s/he is successful, even with part of a word. With this set of words it is important to discuss the spelling rule: with a word that ends in a consonant then **y** is changed to **ie** when the ending **d** or **s** is added.

- Ensure that the child has seen each word correctly written before asking him/her to attempt to write the words in the appropriate places in the sentences. The sentences provided include quite complex words and the child will need some support in reading them by blending the phonemes.

- Encourage the child to make sense of the sentences so that the task of inserting words is made easier.

- As an additional activity you could make up some extra sentences together using some of the target words and point at these words as you say them e.g. *My little brother cried when he tried to swim. "Why did you cry?" I said to him.*

- You could write one of the sentences for the child to copy. Encourage him/her to write clearly, following the school's handwriting policy for letter formation, and to start the sentence with a capital letter and to end it with a full stop. Notice the use of speech marks in the second example sentence above. When looking at this sentence with the child point out that the speech marks surround the actual words spoken, not the whole sentence, and that there is a question mark, because it is a question, before the closing speech marks.

Worksheet 3c

- This sheet includes the seven target words with the phoneme /ie/, together with an extra word, *been*. The extra word is a useful high frequency word and can be used for an 'odd one out' activity.

- This sheet could be copied for display purposes but can also be used to provide the child with extra practice in writing the words. There are three writing lines for each word, enabling the child to use large and smaller writing. You may like to write each word on the first of the two smaller writing lines so that the child can copy your writing in the correct style used by your school.

TARGET WORDS

cry	cries	cried	try
tries	tried	why	been

Andrew Brodie: Supporting Phonics & Spelling © A & C Black Publishers Ltd. 2006

3b **Name:** _____ **Date:** _____

What sounds do the letters make?

c r t y ie s d wh

★ Listen to your teacher. Write the words in the word bank.

WORD BANK

_____ _____ _____

_____ _____ _____

_____ _____ _____

★ Use the correct words to fill the gaps in these sentences.

Tom _____ to ride his bike
but the tyre was flat.

The baby began to _____
because it was hungry.

★ Now write two or three sentences of your own. Make sure
that you include some of the words from the word bank.

_____
_____
_____
_____
_____

Name: **Date:**

Words for today

cry _____ _____

cries _____ _____

cried _____ _____

try _____ _____

tries _____ _____

tried _____ _____

why _____ _____

been _____ _____

4a

Teacher's notes

Worksheet 4a

- Photocopy this page and ask the child to cut out the target words.

- Discuss the words and what each word means. Help the child to read them by blending the phonemes. Ask him/her to identify the sounds in some of the words, the /k/, /ae/ and /k/ in the word *cake*, for example. Discuss the fact that the final **e**, in most of the words, is making the letter **a** 'say its name'.

- Point out that the word *paper* is an 'odd one out' as it is a two syllable word and the others are all single syllables but the letter **e** is still making the **a** say its name.

- Practise breaking words into syllables, perhaps using the child's own name. Remind the child of other two syllable words, especially *going, today, dinner* and *baby*. Introduce the word *alien* – can the child hear the three syllables? Can the child hear all the phonemes in this word? There are five: /ae/, /l/, /ee/, /u/ and /n/. Do not show the child the phonemes written in this way but encourage him/her to listen to them. This is an important element of segmenting words into phonemes to make spelling easier.

Worksheet 4b

- Dictate the following sentences to the child:

  I am going to make a cake today.
  Take a sheet of paper from the desk.
  The alien came from space to play a game.
  The baby made a mess with its dinner.

- As an additional activity you could make up some oral sentences together using some of the target words and point at these words as you say them.

- You could write one of the sentences for the child to copy. Encourage him/her to write clearly, following the school's handwriting policy for letter formation, and to start each sentence with a capital letter and to end it with a full stop.

Worksheet 4c

- This sheet includes the eight target words with the phoneme /ae/. It could be copied for display purposes but can also be used to provide the child with extra practice in writing the words. There are three writing lines for each word, enabling the child to use large and smaller writing. You could write each word on the first of the two smaller writing lines so that the child can copy your writing in the correct style used by your school.

TARGET WORDS

cake	came	game	take
make	made	paper	space

Listen to your teacher. Write the sentences.

Andrew Brodie: Supporting Phonics & Spelling © A & C Black Publishers Ltd. 2006

Name: **Date:**

Words for today

cake _____ _____

came _____ _____

game _____ _____

take _____ _____

make _____ _____

made _____ _____

paper _____ _____

space _____ _____

5a

Phonemes

Consonants: /s/,/k/ (as grapheme c), /m/,/p/,/t/,/f/
Vowels: /a/,/ar/,/ue/,/u/,/er/

Target words

scalp, scamp, scar, scoop, scoot, scooter, scuff, scum

Teacher's notes

Worksheet 5a

- Photocopy this page and ask the child to cut out the target words.

- Discuss the words and what each word means. Help the child to read them by blending the phonemes. Ask him/her to identify the sounds in some of the words, the /s/, /k/, /a/, /m/ and /p/ in the word *scamp*, for example

- Ask the child what there is about the word *scooter* that makes it different from the other words. Accept all sensible answers although the one you are looking for is that *scooter* has two syllables whereas the others are all one-syllable words.

- Explain to the child that having looked very carefully at the target words s/he will be trying to write them unaided on the writing lines provided.

Worksheet 5b

- Help the child to segment the words into their phonemes by dictating the words **scalp, scamp, scar, scoop, scoot, scooter, scuff, scum** several times very slowly.

- Next, the appropriate words should be written in the correct places in the sentences. Help the child to read each sentence, discussing which word will make best sense in the space.

- After completing this you may wish the child to copy out the complete sentences. This should be done as neatly as possible following the school's handwriting policy. Remind the child to copy the correct punctuation.

- As an additional activity you could make up some oral sentences together using some of the target words and pointing at these words on the sheet as you say them, e.g. *The boy liked riding on his new scooter. Try not to scuff your shoes in the playground*.

- You could also make a bank of **sc** words with the child, e.g. *scab, scare, scales*. This will also provide an opportunity to use a dictionary to check the spellings of the suggested words and to discuss the fact that some words that sound the same at the beginning *skate, school,* etc. have different spellings.

Worksheet 5c

- This sheet includes the eight target words. It can be copied for display purposes, but can also be used to provide the child with extra practice in writing the words. There are three writing lines for each word, enabling the child to use both large and smaller writing. You could write each word on the first of the two smaller writing lines so that the child can copy your writing in the correct style used by your school.

TARGET WORDS

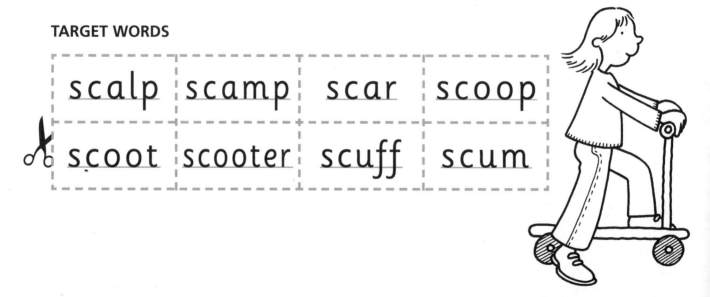

scalp · scamp · scar · scoop

scoot · scooter · scuff · scum

Name: **Date:**

What sounds do the letters make?

s   c   m   p   t   ff   a   ar   oo

★ Listen to your teacher. Write the words.

WORD BANK

★ Use the correct words from the word bank to fill the spaces in these sentences. Then copy the sentences.

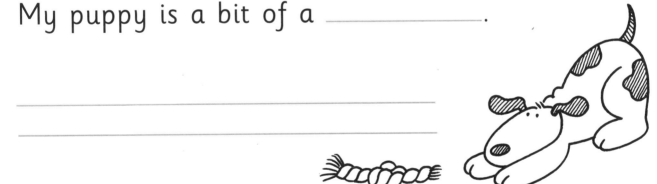

My puppy is a bit of a _____.

_____

_____

Jed ate a large _____ of ice cream.

_____

_____

Name: _____ **Date:** _____

Words for today

scalp   _____   _____

scamp   _____   _____

scar   _____   _____

scoop   _____   _____

scoot   _____   _____

scooter   _____   _____

scuff   _____   _____

scum   _____   _____

Andrew Brodie: Supporting Phonics & Spelling © A & C Black Publishers Ltd. 2006

6a

Phonemes
Consonants: /s/,/n/,/l/,/f/,/p/,/z/,/g/,/k/
Vowels: /oe/,/ae/,/a/,/i/,/u/,/ee/

Target words
snail, snake, snap, sneeze, sniff, snip, snow, snug

Teacher's notes

Worksheet 6a
- Photocopy this page and ask the child to cut out the target words.
- Discuss the words and what each word means. Help the child to read them by blending the phonemes. Ask him/her to identify the sounds in some of the words, the /s/, /n/, /ae/ and /k/ in the word *snake*, for example. Encourage the child to notice that the words all begin with the consonant cluster **sn**.

Worksheet 6b
- Help the child to read the clues and to select the correct words to go with them. S/he should write neatly using clear handwriting in line with the school's handwriting policy.
- On the lower part of the page is a humorous picture for labelling with the words from the word bank. Some of these words are being used for the second time on this page, so it is important that the child does not cross out words from the bank when completing the first part of the sheet. You could cover the word bank to encourage the child to attempt to spell each word without looking. S/he will need to say the word aloud several times to segment it into its phonemes.
- An additional activity could be to make up some sentences using the target words e.g. *Jay felt very snug wrapped in his duvet. A dog likes to sniff things as he walks along the road.*
- You could also make a bank of **sn** words with the child, e.g. *snoop, snare, snout, snarl, snatch, sneaky.* Encourage the child to use a dictionary to check the spelling of these words.

Worksheet 6c
- This sheet includes the eight target words. It can be copied for display purposes, but can also be used to provide the child with extra practice in writing the words. There are three writing lines for each word, enabling the child to use both large and smaller writing. You could write each word on the first of the two smaller writing lines so that the child can copy your writing in the correct style used by your school.

TARGET WORDS

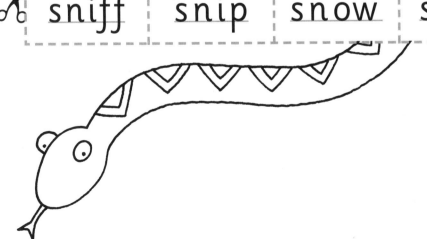

| snail | snake | snap | sneeze |
| sniff | snip | snow | snug |

Name: _____ **Date:** _____

Look at the words in the word bank.
Read them to your teacher.

WORD BANK

snail	snake	snap	sneeze
sniff	snip	snow	snug

★ Write the correct word by each clue.

This falls from the sky _____

A long creature with no legs _____

A small creature with a shell _____

A simple game played with cards _____

★ Now use words from the bank to label the picture.

aahchoo!

Name: _____ **Date:** _____

Words for today

snail _____ _____

snake _____ _____

snap _____ _____

sneeze _____ _____

sniff _____ _____

snip _____ _____

snow _____ _____

snug _____ _____

	Learning objective	
7a	**Phonemes** **Consonants:** /n/,/z/,/t/,/w/,/k/,/s/,/l/,/p/, /g/,/h/,/m/,/b/,/r/,/j/ **Vowels:** /oe/	**Target words** nose, note, woke, slope, home, broke, globe, joke

Teacher's notes

Worksheet 7a

- Photocopy this page and ask the child to cut out the target words.

- Discuss the words and what each word means. Help the child to read them by blending the phonemes. Encourage him/her to look at each word carefully and notice the split digraph o_e at the end of each word. Explain that this has the effect of making the sound /oe/. Note that in this set of words *home* has been included as it is a high frequency word.

Worksheet 7b

- On this sheet there are six pictures with sentences. Each sentence has one word missing. With appropriate support, the child should use his/her phonic skills and knowledge of context to pick the correct word to fit into each space. Whilst this activity has been designed for the appropriate word to be stuck on, you might prefer the child to write the word instead. If this approach is adopted, allow the child enough time to look at each word carefully and to attempt to write it in the space from memory, then to check the accuracy against the printed copy. Help the child segment the words into their phonemes by saying each word several times very slowly.

- On completing this task, the words *joke* and *home* will be left over. The child can then be asked to invent sentences containing those words e.g. *The children went home after school. My joke made everybody laugh.* This work can be purely oral or you could write a sentence for the child to copy, in line with the handwriting policy at your school.

- As an extra activity the child could use this work as a starting point for making a joke book. Each child can contribute one (possibly illustrated) written joke. These can be made into a joke book for the whole group to enjoy. If choosing to do this, give children appropriate help with spelling and presentation, encouraging the use of phonic skills. Point out words that use phonemes already covered in this book.

Worksheet 7c

- This sheet includes the eight target words. It can be copied for display purposes, but can also be used to provide the child with extra practice in writing the words. There are three writing lines for each word, enabling the child to use both large and smaller writing. You could write each word on the first of the two smaller writing lines so that the child can copy your writing in the correct style used by your school.

TARGET WORDS

nose	note	woke	slope
home	broke	globe	joke

Use the target words words to complete the labels for the pictures.

This is a _____ .

The boy ran
down the _____ .

I have a _____
on my face.

I _____ up
in the morning.

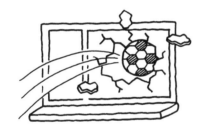

He _____ the
window.

She wrote a _____ .

★ Make up a sentence for each of the words you have got left.
Tell your teacher the sentences.

_____
_____
_____
_____

Andrew Brodie: Supporting Phonics & Spelling © A & C Black Publishers Ltd. 2006

Name: _____ **Date:** _____

Words for today

_____

nose _____ _____

note _____ _____

woke _____ _____

slope _____ _____

home _____ _____

broke _____ _____

globe _____ _____

joke _____ _____

Andrew Brodie: Supporting Phonics & Spelling © A & C Black Publishers Ltd. 2006

8a

Learning objective

Phonemes
Consonants: /s/,/m/,/l/,/t/,/sh/,/k/,/th/, /g/,/ng/
Vowels: /or/,/e/,/ar/,/a/,/oe/,/ue/,/i/,/ie/

Target words
small, smell, smart, smash, smoke, smile, smooth, going

Teacher's notes

Worksheet 8a

- Photocopy this page and ask the child to cut out the target words.

- Discuss the words and what each word means. Help the child to read them by blending the phonemes. Ask him/her to identify the sounds in some of the words, the /s/, /m/, /ar/ and /t/ in the word *smart*, for example. Point out that the word *going* is the 'odd one out'.

Worksheet 8b

- Dictate the following words to the child: **smell, small, smart, smash, smoke, smile, smooth, going**. Showing the cut-out target words to the child and then covering them while you dictate can be a very effective technique. S/he may need some help in segmenting each word into its phonemes to make it easier to spell. Say each word repeatedly and slowly, encouraging the child to hear the separate sounds. It is important that the child is fully supported and given lots of praise where they are successful even with part of a word.

- With this set of words it is important to discuss the consonant cluster **sm** which is at the beginning of all but the final word. The child should be made aware that *going* has been included because it is a word they will come across frequently in their writing.

- Ensure that the child has seen each word correctly written before asking him/her to attempt to write the words in the appropriate places in the sentences.

- When the child makes sentences of his/her own, provide all the support needed with spelling and punctuation. Encourage him/her to write clearly following the school's handwriting policy.

Worksheet 8c

- This sheet includes the seven target words with the consonant cluster **sm**, together with the extra high frequency word *going*. The extra word can also be used for an 'odd one out' activity.

- This sheet could be copied for display purposes but can also be used to provide children with extra practice in writing the words. There are three writing lines for each word, enabling the child to use large and smaller writing. You could write each word on the first of the two smaller lines so that the child can copy your writing in the correct style used by your school.

TARGET WORDS

| small | smell | smart | smash |
| smoke | smile | smooth | going |

Name: **Date:**

Listen to your teacher. Write the words.

WORD BANK

_____   _____   _____

_____   _____   _____

_____   _____

★ Use the correct words to fill in the gaps in these sentences.

There was _____ coming

out of the chimney.

She is _____ out to play.

★ Now write two sentences of your own. Make sure that you include some of the words from the word bank.

_____

_____

_____

_____

Andrew Brodie: Supporting Phonics & Spelling © A & C Black Publishers Ltd. 2006

Words for today

small _____ _____

smell _____ _____

smart _____ _____

smash _____ _____

smoke _____ _____

smile _____ _____

smooth _____ _____

going _____

Learning objective

Phonemes
Consonants: /k/ (as grapheme c), /b/,/j/,/n/,/f/,/l/,/t/, /r/,/d/,/z/ (as grapheme s), /g/
Vowels: /ue/,/oo/

Target words
cube, flute, June, rude, tube, use, used, good

Teacher's notes

Worksheet 9a

- Photocopy this page and ask the child to cut out the target words.

- Discuss the words and what each word means. Help the child to read them by blending the phonemes. Ask him/her to identify the sounds in some of the words, the /k/, /ue/, and /b/ in the word *cube*, for example. Point out that the word *good* is the 'odd one out'.

Worksheet 9b

- Dictate the following words to the child: **cube, flute, June rude, tube, use, used, good**. Showing the cut-out target words to the child then covering them while you dictate can be a very effective technique. Point out the capital letter at the beginning of *June* and remind the child that names should always begin with a capital even when they are not at the start of a sentence. S/he may need some help in segmenting each word into its phonemes to make it easier to spell. Say each word repeatedly and slowly, encouraging the child to hear the separate sounds. It is important that the child is fully supported and given lots of praise where s/he is successful even with part of a word.

- With this set of words it is important to discuss the u_e digraph that occurs in all the words except the word *good*. Children should know that *good* has been included because it is a high frequency word they will often need in their writing.

- The child can then use the words s/he has written to complete the picture labelling and sentence completion activity.

- An additional activity could be to identify the two words not used in the lower part of the page (i.e. *use* and *rude*) and to make up sentences that have those words in e.g. *I like to use the computer. It is rude to stick out your tongue.* It is important that children know when to use the word *use* and when to use the word *used*. The high frequency word *good* can be used for an 'odd one out' activity.

Worksheet 9c

- This sheet includes the eight target words. It can be copied for display purposes, but can also be used to provide the child with extra practice in writing the words. There are three writing lines for each word, enabling the child to use both large and smaller writing. You could write each word on the first of the two smaller writing lines so that the child can copy your writing in the correct style used by your school.

TARGET WORDS

cube | flute | June | rude

tube | use | used | good

Andrew Brodie: Supporting Phonics & Spelling © A & C Black Publishers Ltd. 2006

Name: _____ **Date:** _____

Listen to your teacher. Write the words.

WORD BANK

_____   _____   _____

_____   _____   _____

_____   _____

Put the correct word under each picture.

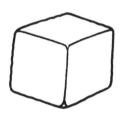   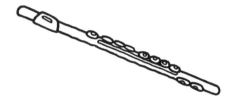   

_____   _____   _____

Put the correct word in each sentence.

The month before July is _____.

I am very _____ at spelling.

I _____ to be eight but now I am nine.

Name: **Date:**

Words for today

cube

flute

June

rude

tube

use

used

good

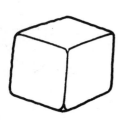

Andrew Brodie: Supporting Phonics & Spelling © A & C Black Publishers Ltd. 2006

10a

Learning objective

Phonemes
Consonants: /s/,/p/,/n/,/t/,/l/,/d/,/k/
Vowels: /ue/,/or/,/ar/,/e/,/ee/,/ae/,/i/

Target words
spoon, sport, spark, spell,
speed, space, spill, spend

Teacher's notes

Worksheet 10a

- Photocopy this page and ask the child to cut out the target words.

- Discuss the words and what each word means. Help the child to read them by blending the phonemes. Ask him/her to identify the sounds in some of the words, the /s/, /p/, /ue/, and /n/ in the word *spoon*, for example.

Worksheet 10b

- Discuss the words printed at the top of the sheet. Point out the consonant cluster **sp** at the beginning of each one. The child can write each of the words on the given lines.

- Tell the child that the next part of the task will be to listen to each of the words as you say them and to write the word below the correct picture. Ensure that the child covers the words at the top so s/he is prevented from copying. S/he may need some help in segmenting each word into its phonemes to make it easier to spell. Say each word repeatedly and slowly, encouraging the child to hear the separate sounds.

- After dictating the words to label the pictures, let the child check each word that s/he has written against the word at the top of the page – provide help if needed and praise for correct attempts.

- An additional activity could be to make up sentences for some of the words e.g. *I spend my money with speed. Do not spill sugar from the spoon.*

- You could build a bank of **sp** words with the children. This could be used to help them check spellings using a dictionary and encourages them to look for the third letter when doing so. Be sure to also include words with the **sp** cluster occurring in the middle or at the end of a word. Your word bank might include the following: *inspect, gasp, splatter, spray, split, despair, lisp.*

Worksheet 10c

- This sheet includes the eight target words. It can be copied for display purposes, but can also be used to provide the child with extra practice in writing the words. There are three writing lines for each word, enabling the child to use both large and smaller writing. You could write each word on the first of the two smaller writing lines so that the child can copy your writing in the correct style used by your school.

TARGET WORDS

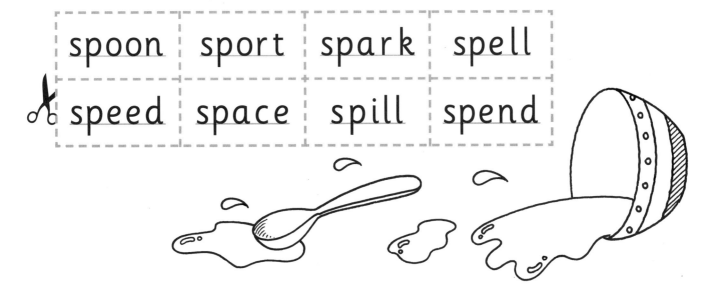

Name: **Date:**

Look at the words. Write the words.

spark   sport   spend

_____   _____   _____

spill   spoon   space

_____   _____   _____

spell   speed

_____   _____

Your teacher will say each of the words.
Write each word below the correct picture.

_____   _____   _____

_____   _____   _____

_____   _____

Andrew Brodie: Supporting Phonics & Spelling © A & C Black Publishers Ltd. 2006

Name: _____ **Date:** _____

Words for today

spoon _____ _____

sport _____ _____

spark _____ _____

spell _____ _____

speed _____ _____

space _____ _____

spill _____ _____

spend _____ _____

Learning objective

Phonemes
Consonants: /s/,/p/,/t/,/d/,/n/,/h/, /m/,/ng/
Vowels: /i/,/o/,/oe/

Target words
spot, spotted, spotting, spin, spinning, spit, spitting, home

Teacher's notes

Worksheet 11a

- Photocopy this page and ask the child to cut out the target words.

- Discuss the words and what each word means. Help the child to read them by blending the phonemes. Ask him/her to identify the sounds in some of the words, the /s/, /p/, /i/ and /n/ in the word *spin*, for example. Ask the child to notice the doubling of the final letter on the words when endings **ing** or **ed** are added.

- Can the child spot the word that is the 'odd one out'? Explain that the word *home* has been included as it is a word s/he may need to write frequently so it's important to know how to spell it correctly. The children have met this word before in Set 7.

Worksheet 11b

- Explain to the child that having looked carefully at the words, s/he will be trying to write them unaided on the writing lines provided.

- Next, the appropriate words should be written in the correct places in the sentences on this sheet. Help the child to read each sentence and discuss which word will make best sense in the space. Pronounce each word clearly so the child is able to write the word correctly. S/he may need some help in segmenting each word into its phonemes to make it easier to spell. Say each word repeatedly and slowly, encouraging the child to hear the separate sounds.

- After completing the sentences you could ask the children to copy them out. This should be done as neatly as possible following the school's handwriting policy. Remind the child to copy the correct punctuation as shown in the printed sentences.

- As an additional activity you could make up some extra sentences together using some of the target words and point at these words on the sheet as you say them. e.g. *Spitting is not a polite thing to do. There is a spot of dirt on my shirt.*

Worksheet 11c

- This sheet includes the eight target words. It can be copied for display purposes, but can also be used to provide the child with extra practice in writing the words. There are three writing lines for each word, enabling the child to use both large and smaller writing. You may like to write each word on the first of the two smaller writing lines so that the child can copy your writing in the correct style used by your school.

TARGET WORDS

| spot | spotted | spotting | spin |
| spinning | spit | spitting | home |

Name: **Date:**

Listen to your teacher. Write the words.

WORD BANK

Use the correct words to fill the spaces in these sentences. Then copy the sentences.

I will go _____ after school.

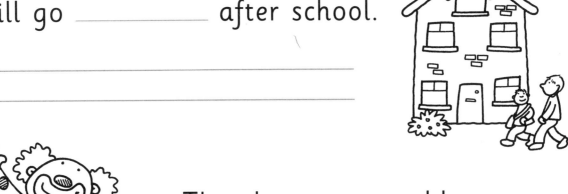

_____

_____

The clown wore a blue and pink _____ coat.

_____

_____

The spider was busy _____ a web.

_____

_____

Name: _____ **Date:** _____

Words for today

spot _____ _____

spotted _____ _____

spotting _____ _____

spin _____ _____

spinning _____ _____

spit _____ _____

spitting _____ _____

home _____ _____

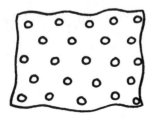

Andrew Brodie: Supporting Phonics & Spelling © A & C Black Publishers Ltd. 2006

12a

Learning objective	
Phonemes Consonants: /s/,/t/,/r/,/ng/,/k/,/m/,/g/,/l/ Vowels: /i/,/o/,/ie/,/or/,/ae/,/ee/,/u/	**Target words** string, strong, strike, straw, stray, street, stream, struggle

Teacher's notes

Worksheet 12a

- Photocopy this page and ask the child to cut out the target words.

- Discuss the words and what each word means. Help the child to read them by blending the phonemes. Ask him/her to identify the sounds in some of the words, the /s/, /t/, /r/, /i/ and /ng/ in the word *string*, for example.

Worksheet 12b

- Explain to the child that having looked carefully at the words, s/he will be trying to write them unaided on the writing lines provided.

- Next, the appropriate words should be written in the correct places in the picture labels. Help the child to read each label. Discuss which word will make best sense in the space and pronounce each word clearly so the child can write the word correctly. S/he may need some help in segmenting each word into its phonemes to make it easier to spell. Say each word repeatedly and slowly, encouraging the child to hear the separate sounds.

- An additional activity would be to make up sentences that include some of the target words e.g. *The stray dog ran down the street. A piece of string fell into the stream. Strike a match to start a fire.*

- You could also ask the child to write down one of the sentences in the handwriting style used by your school.

Worksheet 12c

- This sheet includes the eight target words. It can be copied for display purposes, but can also be used to provide the child with extra practice in writing the words. There are three writing lines for each word, enabling the child to use both large and smaller writing. You could write each word on the first of the two smaller writing lines so that the child can copy your writing in the correct style used by your school.

TARGET WORDS

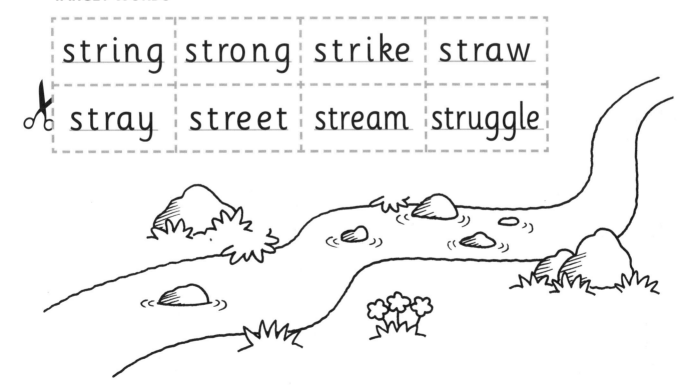

Name: _____   **Date:** _____

Listen to your teacher. Write the words.

WORD BANK

_____   _____   _____

_____   _____   _____

_____   _____

★ Use the correct words to complete the picture labels.

Bales of _____.

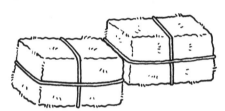

A busy _____.

A ball of _____.

A _____ dog.

★ Write a sentence using some **str** words.

_____

_____

_____

_____

Name: _____ **Date:** _____

Words for today

string _____ _____

strong _____ _____

strike _____ _____

straw _____ _____

stray _____ _____

street _____ _____

stream _____ _____

struggle _____ _____

Learning objective	
Phonemes Consonants: /s/,/w/,/m/,/n/,/p/,/ng/,/t/ Vowels: /i/,/a/,/o/,/ee/,/ue/	**Target words** swim, swam, swan, swap, swing, sweet, sweep, swoop

Teacher's notes

Worksheet 13a

- Photocopy this page and ask the child to cut out the target words.

- Discuss the words and what each word means. Help the child to read them by blending the phonemes. Encourage the child to notice that all the words have the consonant cluster **sw** at the beginning. Look particularly at the vowels in each of the words, as this will help children with their spelling. Focus on the fact that the letter **a** in *swan* and *swap* is the phoneme /o/.

Worksheet 13b

- Explain to the child that the target words on this sheet are shown, but without vowels.

- Read each of the words to the child allowing him/her time to insert the vowels. S/he may need some help in segmenting each word into its phonemes to make it easier to spell. Say each word repeatedly and slowly, encouraging the child to hear the separate sounds.

- In the second part of the worksheet the child should read the clues and then insert the correct word to match each clue.

- An additional activity would be to make up clues for the words *swing, swam, swap, swoop*. You could also help the child to make up tongue twisters using other words beginning with **sw**. S/he could use a dictionary to find a selection of words suitable for this e.g. *Swim swan swim. So the swan swam. You could switch or swap your swing. Swooping swallows see swift swans swimming.*

Worksheet 13c

- This sheet includes the eight target words. It can be copied for display purposes, but can also be used to provide the child with extra practice in writing the words. There are three writing lines for each word, enabling the child to use both large and smaller writing. You could write each word on the first of the two smaller writing lines so that the child can copy your writing in the correct style used by your school.

TARGET WORDS

swim	swam	swan	swap
swing	sweet	sweep	swoop

Name: **Date:**

Listen to your teacher.
Put the missing letters into the words.

s w __ __ p   s w __ __ t   s w __ __ p   s w __ n g

s w __ n   s w __ m   s w __ m   s w __ p

★ Read the clues.
Put the correct word by each clue.

Use a broom to do this: _____

A large white water bird: _____

The taste of sugar: _____

A way to move through water: _____

★ Can you make up clues for the words swing, swam, swap, swoop?

swing _____

swam   _____

swap   _____

swoop _____

Andrew Brodie: Supporting Phonics & Spelling © A & C Black Publishers Ltd. 2006

Name: **Date:**

Words for today

swim _____ _____

swam _____ _____

swan _____ _____

swap _____ _____

swing _____ _____

sweet _____ _____

sweep _____ _____

swoop _____ _____

14a

Learning objective	
Phonemes **Consonants:** /t/,/w/,/l/,/v/,/n/,/g/ **Vowels:** /ee/,/e/,/i/,/ur/,/ue/	**Target words** tweet, twelve, twenty, twig, twin, twirl, twist, two

Teacher's notes

Worksheet 14a

- Photocopy this page and ask the child to cut out the target words.

- Discuss the words and what each word means. Help the child to read them by blending the phonemes. Ask him/her to identify the sounds in some of the words, the /t/, /w/, /ee/, and /t/ in the word *tweet*, for example.

Worksheet 14b

- Look at all the words at the top of the sheet. Read each one to the child. Ask him/her to pick the 'odd one out'. Accept and praise each reasonable answer though the answer you are looking for is that *two* is the 'odd one out', as you cannot hear the **w** in it. Explain that when *two* is spelled this way it stands for the number two. Now ask the child to write each of the words on the writing lines.

- Explain to the child that the next part of the task will be to listen to each of the words as you say them and to write the word below the correct picture.

- Ensure that the child covers the words at the top so s/he is not able to copy them. S/he may need some help in segmenting each word into its phonemes to make it easier to spell. Say each word repeatedly and slowly, encouraging the child to hear the separate sounds.

- After dictating the words to label the pictures, let the child check each word that s/he has written against the word at the top of the page. Provide help where needed and praise correct attempts.

- An additional activity could be to make up sentences for the words e.g. *Twenty-two twigs fell from a tree. My twin birds go tweet tweet.*

- You could also build a bank of **tw** words with the child. This could be used to help the child check spellings in a dictionary and encourages him/her to look for the third letter when doing so. Your word bank might include the following: *twang, tweak, twitch, entwine.*

Worksheet 14c

- This sheet includes the eight target words. It can be copied for display purposes, but can also be used to provide the child with extra practice in writing the words. There are three writing lines for each word, enabling the child to use both large and smaller writing. You could write each word on the first of the two smaller writing lines so that the child can copy your writing in the correct style used by your school.

TARGET WORDS

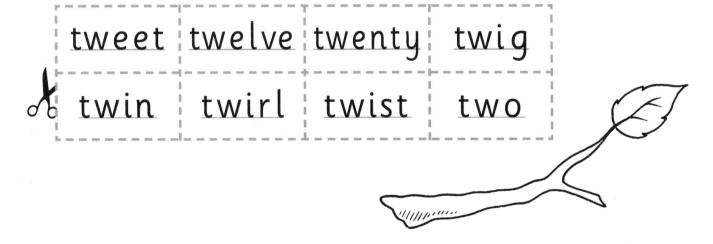

tweet	twelve	twenty	twig
twin	twirl	twist	two

Andrew Brodie: Supporting Phonics & Spelling © A & C Black Publishers Ltd. 2006

Name: _____ **Date:** _____

Look at the words. Write the words.

twin	twelve	two
_____	_____	_____

tweet	twenty	twig
_____	_____	_____

twirl	twist
_____	_____

★ Your teacher will say each of the words.
Write each word below the correct picture.

_____   _____   _____

_____   _____   _____

_____   _____

Name: _____   **Date:** _____

Words for today

tweet _____   _____

twelve _____   _____

twenty _____   _____

twig _____   _____

twin _____   _____

twirl _____   _____

twist _____   _____

two _____   _____

15a

Learning objective

Phonemes
Consonants: /s/,/k/ (as grapheme c),
/r/,/p/,/b/,/l/,/m/,/n/
Vowels: /a/,/ae/,/i/,/ee/,/u/

Target words
scrap, scrape, scrabble, scribble,
scream, screen, scrub, scramble

Teacher's notes

Worksheet 15a

- Photocopy this page and ask the child to cut out the target words.

- Discuss the words and what each word means. Help the child to read them by blending the phonemes. Ask him/her to identify the sounds in some of the words, the /s/, /k/, /r/, /a/ and /p/ in the word *scrap*, for example. The words *scrap* and *scrape* provide excellent revision of the effect of the 'final e'. In the word *scrap* the letter **a** makes the /a/ phoneme. In the word *scrape* the letter **a** works with the final **e** to give the split digraph a_e making the phoneme /ae/.

- Revise the idea of syllables. Can the child identify which words have one syllable and which words have two? This is a very important speaking and listening activity that helps children with the skill of segmenting.

Worksheet 15b

- Dictate the words **scrap, scrape, scrabble, scribble, scream, screen, scrub, scramble** in random order for the child to create the word bank. S/he may need some help in segmenting each word into its phonemes to make it easier to spell. Say each word repeatedly and slowly, encouraging the child to hear the separate sounds.

- On the lower part of the sheet is the sentence: *A scrap of paper fell on the floor.* This sentence should be read with the child who should pick out the word *scrap* as one of the target words.

- Explain that some writing lines are provided for writing three complete sentences, each of which should contain one of the **scr** words. Remind the child to begin each sentence with a capital letter and complete it with a full stop.

Worksheet 15c

- This sheet includes the eight target words. It can be copied for display purposes, but can also be used to provide the child with extra practice in writing the words. There are three writing lines for each word, enabling the child to use both large and smaller writing. You could write each word on the first of the two smaller writing lines so that the child can copy your writing in the correct style used by your school.

TARGET WORDS

scrap	scrape	scrabble	scribble
scream	screen	scrub	scramble

Andrew Brodie: Supporting Phonics & Spelling © A & C Black Publishers Ltd. 2006

Name: **Date:**

Listen to your teacher. Write the words.

WORD BANK

★ Look at this sentence.

A scrap of paper fell on the floor.

★ Write three sentences. Make sure that each sentence has one of the **scr** words in it.

Words for today

scrap

scrape

scrabble

scribble

scream

screen

scrub

scramble

If you said srap paper it means spare

It means like I scape off the mud with a shovel

I's a game on the letter played on a board

scribble means crossing out a lot

screaming is when you shout a lot

screen mean like a TV screen

scrub means like scrubing the car

it means like scramble egg

I would like some scrap paper please.

Scrape off the mud.

thing we like to eat

pear to R____

AAAAAh! there's a spider

Look at the movie screen

I scrubing the lorry I'd like scramble egg on toast

Learning objective	
Phonemes **Consonants:** /sh/,/r/,/d/,/g/,/ng/,/k/,/l/, /b/,/n/ **Vowels:** /e/,/i/,/u/,/ow/	**Target words** shred, shredded, shredding, shrug, shrink, shrill, shrub, now

Teacher's notes

Worksheet 16a

- Photocopy this page and ask the child to cut out the target words.

- Discuss the words and what each word means. Help the child to read them by blending the phonemes. Ask him/her to identify the sounds in some of the words, the /sh/, /r/, /e/ and /d/ in the word *shred*, for example. Point out the doubling of the letter **d** when *shred* becomes *shredded* or *shredding*. Ask the child which word is the 'odd one out' and why.

- Explain that *now* has been included in the word list as it is another word that is likely to be used frequently in their writing.

Worksheet 16b

- Photocopy this sheet and then slowly and clearly dictate the following sentences. The child may need some help in segmenting each word into its phonemes to make it easier to spell. Say each word repeatedly and slowly, encouraging the child to hear the separate sounds.

  I will shred my paper now.
  Mum got a new shrub for the garden.
  The bird had a very shrill cry.
  "How should I know?" said the boy with a shrug.

- When looking at the completed sentences it is important to praise all attempts at correct punctuation, particularly the speech marks and question mark included in the final sentence.

Worksheet 16c

- This sheet includes the eight target words. This sheet can be copied for display purposes, but can also be used to provide the child with extra practice in writing the words. There are three writing lines for each word, enabling the child to use both large and smaller writing. You could write each word on the first of the two smaller writing lines so that the child can copy your writing in the correct style used by your school.

TARGET WORDS

shred	shredded	shredding	shrug
shrink	shrill	shrub	now

16b Name: _____ Date: _____

Listen to your teacher. Write the sentences.

_____

_____

_____

_____

_____

_____

_____

_____

_____

_____

_____

_____

_____

_____

_____

_____

Andrew Brodie: Supporting Phonics & Spelling © A & C Black Publishers Ltd. 2006

Name: **Date:**

Words for today

shred _____ _____

shredded _____ _____

shredding _____ _____

shrug _____ _____

shrink _____ _____

shrill _____ _____

shrub _____ _____

now _____ _____

17a

Phonemes
Consonants: /th/,/r/,/l/,/t/,/d/,/n/
Vowels: /ee/,/oe/,/ue/,/i/,/e/,/ow/

Target words
three, throw, through, threw, thrill, throat, thread, down

Teacher's notes

Worksheet 17a

- Photocopy this page and ask the child to cut out the target words.

- Discuss the words and what each word means. Help the child to read them by blending the phonemes. Ask him/her to identify the sounds in some of the words, the /th/, /r/, /i/, and /l/ in the word *thrill*, for example.

- Encourage the child to notice that all the words feature the consonant cluster **thr** at the beginning. Ask the child to pick out the word that is the 'odd one out'. Explain that *down* is another important word, as s/he will come across it frequently in their writing.

- Look particularly at the combination of vowels in each of the words as this will help with its spelling. Focus on *threw* and *through* and ensure that the child understands the different meaning of these two words.

Worksheet 17b

- Explain to the child that the target words are shown, but without vowels. Read each of the words to the child allowing him/her time to insert the vowels. S/he may need some help in segmenting each word into its phonemes to make it easier to spell. Say each word repeatedly and slowly, encouraging the child to hear the separate sounds.

- The child may notice that two of the words look identical when the vowel is missing. It is useful to use this example to explain the importance of using the correct vowel to ensure the correct meaning of a word.

- In the second part of the sheet the child should read the clues then insert the correct word to match each clue. An additional activity would be to make up clues for the words, *thrill*, *threw*, *through*, *throw*.

- A further activity could be to investigate other pairs of words that sound the same but have different spellings and meanings (homophones). These might for example include:

  road, rowed, rode　　*pair, pare, pear*
  seen, scene　　　　　*throne, thrown*

Worksheet 17c

- This sheet includes the eight target words. It can be copied for display purposes, but can also be used to provide the child with extra practice in writing the words. There are three writing lines for each word, enabling the child to use both large and smaller writing. You could write each word on the first of the two smaller writing lines so that the child can copy your writing in the correct style used by your school.

TARGET WORDS

three | throw | through | threw
thrill | throat | thread | down

Name: _____   **Date:** _____

Listen to your teacher.
Put the missing letters into the words.

thr __ __   thr__w   thr__w   thr__ __gh

thr__ll   thr__ __t   thr__ __d   d__wn

★ Read the clues.
Put the correct word by each clue.

Use this in a needle
for sewing: _____

The opposite of up: _____

The number between two
and four: _____

Find this in your neck: _____

★ Can you make up clues for the words thrill, threw, through and throw?

thrill   _____

threw   _____

through   _____

throw   _____

Name: **Date:**

Words for today

three _____ _____

throw _____ _____

through _____ _____

threw _____ _____

thrill _____ _____

throat _____ _____

thread _____ _____

down _____ _____

   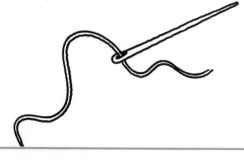

 Andrew Brodie: Supporting Phonics & Spelling © A & C Black Publishers Ltd. 2006

Learning objective	
Phonemes **Consonants:** /s/,/p/,/l/,/r/,/sh/,/t/,/n/, /d/,/ng/,/k/ **Vowels:** /a/,/i/,/e/,/er/,/ae/	**Target words** splash, split, splendid, splinter, spring, spray, spread, sprinkle

Teacher's notes

Worksheet 18a

- Photocopy this page and ask the child to cut out the target words.

- Discuss the words and what each word means. Help the child to read them by blending the phonemes. Ask him/her to identify the sounds in some of the words, the /s/, /p/, /l/, /i/, and /t/ in the word *split*, for example.

- Help him/her to notice that whilst all the words begin with the consonant cluster **sp**, four of them start with the cluster **spr** and the other four start with the cluster **spl**. Explain that these words are longer than many they have encountered so it is very important to focus on how each word is spelt.

Worksheet 18b

- On this sheet the child is asked to put missing letters into words listed in this order: **splash**, **splinter**, **splendid**, **split**, **spray**, **spring**, **spread**, **sprinkle**. Dictate each word and allow ample time for the children to insert the correct letters before going on to the next word. S/he may need some help in segmenting each word into its phonemes to make it easier to spell. Say each word repeatedly and slowly, encouraging the child to hear the separate sounds. Allow him/her to check his/her attempts against the correct spellings on the cut-out words and to make any changes needed.

- The second part of this sheet asks the child to choose the correct words to complete the given sentences. There are writing lines for the child to copy the complete sentences, in the style used by your school and paying attention to correct punctuation.

- An additional activity could be to make up more sentences including any words beginning with **spr** or **spl**, having first used a dictionary to investigate these e.g. *I ate some splendid sprouts for dinner. Sprint past the spruce trees in the spring.*

Worksheet 18c

- This sheet includes the eight target words. It can be copied for display purposes, but can also be used to provide the child with extra practice in writing the words. There are three writing lines for each word, enabling the child to use both large and smaller writing. You could write each word on the first of the two smaller writing lines so that the child can copy your writing in the correct style used by your school.

TARGET WORDS

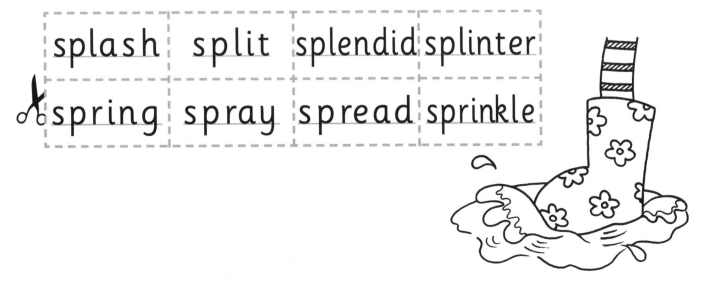

splash | split | splendid | splinter

spring | spray | spread | sprinkle

Name: _____   **Date:** _____

Listen to your teacher.
Put the missing letters in each word.

s p l a s h   S p l i n t e r   s p l e n d i d

s p l i t   S p r ay   s p r i n g

s p r e a d   s p r i n k l e

★ Write the correct word in each sentence.
Copy each sentence on the line.

Dad likes to _____
the flowers with water.

Dad Likes to ~~spay~~ ~~spray~~ sprinkle
the flowers with water

_____

I got a _____ in my finger.

I got a Splinter in
my finger

_____

Andrew Brodie: Supporting Phonics & Spelling © A & C Black Publishers Ltd. 2006

Name: _____ **Date:** _____

Words for today

splash _____ _____

split _____ _____

splendid _____ _____

splinter _____ _____

spring _____ _____

spray _____ _____

spread _____ _____

sprinkle _____ _____

  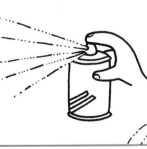 

19a

Learning objective

Phonemes
Consonants: /s/,/k/,/w/,/sh/,/d/,
/t/,/z/,/b/,/l/
Vowels: /o/,/air/,/i/,/ur/,/ee/

Target words
squash, square, squid, squirt,
squeak, squeeze, squabble, squeal

Teacher's notes

Worksheet 19a

- Photocopy this page and ask the child to cut out the target words.

- Discuss the words and what each word means. Help the child to read them by blending the phonemes. Ask him/her to identify the sounds in some of the words, the /s/, /k/, /w/, /o/, and /sh/ in the word *squash*, for example. Discuss the fact that the letter **q** is always followed by a **u**. Look particularly at the combination of vowels in each of the words, as this will help children with their spelling of these words.

Worksheet 19b

- Photocopy this sheet and explain to the child that the target words are shown, but without vowels. Read each of the words **squash**, **square**, **squid**, **squirt**, **squeak**, **squeeze**, **squabble**, **squeal** to the child allowing him/her time to insert the vowels. S/he may need some help in segmenting each word into its phonemes to make it easier to spell. Say each word repeatedly and slowly, encouraging the child to hear the separate sounds. Remind the child that **q** will always be followed by **u**.

- In the lower part of this sheet the child should read the clues then insert the correct word to match each clue. An additional activity would be to make up clues for the words *squeal*, *squabble*, *squirt* and *squash*.

- A further activity could be to investigate building a word bank of words beginning with **squ** e.g. *squirrel, squint, squad, squiggle, squelch*.

Worksheet 19c

- This sheet includes the eight target words. It can be copied for display purposes, but can also be used to provide the child with extra practice in writing the words. There are three writing lines for each word, enabling the child to use both large and smaller writing. You could write each word on the first of the two smaller writing lines so that the child can copy your writing in the correct style used by your school.

TARGET WORDS

| squash | square | squid | squirt |
| squeak | squeeze | squabble | squeal |

Andrew Brodie: Supporting Phonics & Spelling © A & C Black Publishers Ltd. 2006

Name: _____   **Date:** _____

Listen to your teacher.
Put the missing letters into the words.

sq __ __ rt   s q __ __ d   sq __ __ __ z __

sq __ __ b bl __   sq __ __ r __   sq __ __ s h

sq __ __ __ k   sq __ __ __ l

Read the clues.
Write the correct word by each clue.

To press from each side: _____

A mouse makes a sound like this: _____

A shape with four equal sides: _____

A sea creature: _____

Can you make up clues for the words squeal,
squabble, squirt and squash?

squeal   _____

squabble   _____

squirt   _____

squash   _____

Name: _____ **Date:** _____

Words for today

squash

square

squid

squirt

squeak

squeeze

squabble

squeal

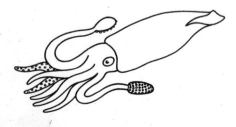
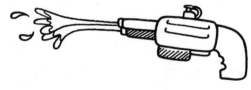

Andrew Brodie: Supporting Phonics & Spelling © A & C Black Publishers Ltd. 2006